Lug Your Careless Body out of t

winner of the IOWA POETRY PRIZE

Lug Your Careless Body out of the Careful Dusk

a poem in fragments

Joshua Marie Wilkinson

UNIVERSITY OF IOWA PRESS   Iowa City

University of Iowa Press, Iowa City 52242

Copyright © 2006 by Joshua Marie Wilkinson

http://www.uiowa.edu/uiowapress

All rights reserved

Printed in the United States of America

Design by Richard Hendel

The University of Iowa Press is a member of Green Press
Initiative and is committed to preserving natural resources.

Printed on acid-free paper

Library of Congress Cataloging-in-Publication Data
Wilkinson, Joshua Marie, 1977–.
Lug your careless body out of the careful dusk: a poem in fragments /
by Joshua Marie Wilkinson.
p.   cm.—(The Iowa poetry prize)
ISBN 0-87745-981-9 (pbk.)
I. Title.   II. Series.
PS3623.15526L84 2006
811'.6—dc22   2005053851

08 09 10 P 5 4 3 2

Lug Your Careless Body out of the Careful Dusk

This book is for my mom and dad,

for J'Lyn,

and in memory of my grandmother

Marie Wilkinson Wilson, 1913–2000

And to feel that the light is a rabbit-light

In which everything is meant for you

And nothing need be explained

—Wallace Stevens, "A Rabbit as King of the Ghosts"

Contents

Acknowledgments

Parts of this book first appeared (often in markedly different forms) in *Barrow Street, Crab Creek Review, Cranky, Crescent Moon, CutBank, DIAGRAM, Harness, Phoebe, Pontoon 8: An Anthology of Washington State Poets,* and *Tarpaulin Sky*. Kindest thanks to the tireless editors of these journals.

Two of these fragments won an Academy of American Poets Prize judged by Ellen Bryant Voigt in 2003 when I attended the University of Arizona, one of which was published on the Tucson Poetry Center's annual broadside. Grateful acknowledgment is made to the Poetry Center, Frances Sjoberg and Christine Krikliwy, and to my friends and mentors at the University of Arizona.

Two sections of this book were published in 2005 by New Michigan Press as a chapbook entitled *A Ghost as King of the Rabbits*, with illustrations by J'Lyn Chapman. Enormous thanks to Ander Monson and the readers and editors at NMP.

Without the help of the following vigilant readers (and friends), this book could not have been completed: J'Lyn Chapman, Christina Mengert, Danielle Dutton, Paul Fattaruso, Julie Doxsee, Marty Riker, and Gregory Howard. Continuous thanks to my teachers: Eleni Sikelianos, Bin Ramke, Laird Hunt, Brian Kiteley, and Elizabeth Robinson. A humongous thank you to Jane Miller and Bruce Beasley, Alison Hawthorne Deming, Boyer Rickel, David Rubin, Solan Jascha Jensen, Zach Zulauf, Scott Lindsay, my brother Jeffrey Wilson, Laura Brian, and Austin Whipple. To Graham Foust for seeing a book in these fragments, to Holly Carver, Allison Thomas, Deidre Woods, Karen Copp, Charlotte Wright, and Brien Woods at the University of Iowa Press for unflagging help. Continued thanks to John and Mary Felstiner, Cole Swensen, Anne Carson, Marjorie Perloff, Richard Greenfield, Kelly Link, Jason Zuzga, Frank Montesonti, Richard Siken, Gwyneth Scally, Allison Maletz, Diane Wiener, Amber Curtis, Karla Kelsey, Joshua Beckman, Christian Hawkey, Travis Nichols, Noah Eli Gordon, Sara Veglahn, Termite, and the indefatigable Tim Rutili and Califone.

A Moth in the Projectorlight

* * *

Even if only in photographs—
a laundry truck, seconds after.
Phone in the apartment ringing
above the accident & a coroner
careful enough to stay speechless
until the wind picks up
& the passersby can smell simply
the blood, like fresh wood or
cut metal.

* * *

A boy of six cups his hands
around a wet moth
as he stands up
in the bathtub
releasing it to the mirrorlight.
Beige wingdust on his palm.

* * *

Yellow. The room is orange
& black also. Water
a whistle, draining in his mother's tub.

* * *

This is the part of the story where
you leave
       & where I come in.
                         Wait
there
       no—
            there
around the corner for the signal:
the greenfinch
your twin sisters will
free from the balcony.

    * * *

Came around
smelling of rye.
Aluminum dust under his
fingernails.

    * * *

Memory opens a little door:
the dark & you listen
with your eyes
& write things in my letter
you'll pretend later
to forget.

* * *

A kid at the mailbox sings that
your brothers are deader than doorlocks,
that your mother lives
in their teeth.

* * *

            City of
no center, broke-lit
from the team of horses
asleep standing
under the great lamps.

* * *

A curse of split melon
on the kitchen counter

draws me out into the snowdrift.
White heat from the boy's breath
& the toy house's tiny doorbell
chimes somehow in the empty room
startling the cat.

* * *

You took your apricot dress to the drycleaners
& left it forever.

Haystink, humming street ruckus, moonlit
thumb-slice—
Each evening I peek into that mailbox
for what my father's unable to tell me
on the edge of my own bed
feeling that
morning will scorch
into the sockets of his arms
& that he is
drinking   sorry again
Anna   sleep
sorry again.

Was it cement truck speed or rickety carousel speed?
Will you give me what's left of her shirt?
From what distance will your coins be counted?

* * *

When the missive arrives
Anna lifts
her blouse, tucks the envelope

   into the front of her blue skirt
& locks herself in the bathroom.

* * *

I like it when the camera stops
outside a door like this
& just waits a moment, listens.

* * *

Lugged the stars
down to pull them through
the riversoup.

* * *

From the porch my father is pissing
into the dust & dark.

Did the movies spoil you early?
Couldn't the river take that man away?
Had you wished for a better entry?

The man slumped wide-eyed
dead at the wheel of the milk truck
isn't enough for a poem until
the ground thaws,
the windshield splatters onto the dash,
into his pleated lap & animals catch
the opened scent.
Montana burned fresh. They nuzzle
& tug him lengthwise
like a dummy
into the goat field
& wish him goodbye.

* * *

Sweaty water, oven belly, brick chin, monster
oarsman, your man square
in the mirror like he's been drinking
the spitty punches.

* * *

Gin Rummy. Your slick way of saying
alright
  like granddad.

* * *

To have come all the way back by
three buses, night mizzle & a little whatchayacallit
to the funeral. Somebody

mistakes your uncle for
your father at the reception
& it occurs to me that even music
wouldn't do this to us
without first
asking for a dance.

The Trick Was to Disappear

* * *

Thieves carry
Lucian's painting of Francis Bacon out
of the museum in a thin paper bag
                    & descend into the stairs
                              under the city.

The trick was
        to disappear
simultaneously
            without words,
                    effort or a glance.

* * *

Bludgeoned light of dusk.
The face of the moon reflected in a shovel.

Peat-rot dusk.
Bluegill & ham-fisted dusk.

Dusk like
your doctor's wooden teeth.

* * *

Sad luck of coins
                    in the dryer. Church songs
or hollering
            behind the conversation
                            on the phone.

* * *

ladder *n*. [*v*. laddering] 1. Two sidepieces of
wood, metal, or rope, joined by rungs at intervals
to form steps for climbing. 2. A wide run in a
stocking or sweater. See also: stepladder,
stairs, companionway, jack ladder, rigging,
fire escape, Jacob's ladder.   —*Webster's New Collegiate Dictionary*, 1959.

* * *

The entry lit with lamps. Pry it
                            gently open.

* * *

The thief of townhall, the drugstore basement
& boatyard thieves.

* * *

Did the stinger break in the belly?
Was there any time for speaking?
Couldn't you hear the fishermen hauling the skiffs in?

* * *

The engine ladder sleeps & silence
falls down as the men play cards.

* * *

Just thirst, the sweet alarm
of bells & furious birds,
a crackling subway-like voice
over the intercom into the backroom
until somebody yells again for quiet.

* * *

Cat burglar, doggie door, tool pouch,
the old ski mask & waterballoon trick.
A bag of sugar for the gas tank.

* * *

As an impatient moon scolds him
the school locker thief
imagines all
the rooms of the house
all at once, each with a member
of the family busy with food
or gossip.

* * *

Even though every little sound
is oceanless, clean & punctured.

* * *

Was the money concealed well enough?
Were the thieves' radios tuned the same?
Did you wait in the phone booth & feign speaking?

* * *

Grease light, burst bulb garage- & box-light,
a boy eases himself under the car, knowing
he'll be caught, yanked out by the legs,
beaten, all three or a fourth.

* * *

A cape of blood
        smeared
into the winter brushfield,

                tree racket
        over the dishwashers on a break
        behind the drive-through.

* * *

Each evening
I rearrange my bedroom.
It's nearly clockwork.
The song's violins unspool as I pull
the furniture around, break a sweat,
trap myself in little corners.

* * *

Soon enough
beach lice
              will scour out
        the eyes of the doe
& I will
      return to heave
          the lead bathtub out
   from under the house
& finish
      like a cigarette
            the story.

* * *

Boy-scatter in the market,
moths awake inside the piano.

* * *

Surely you remember the legendary earthquake.

* * *

A little bit of Christmas in your eyes,
stuck to your red lips.

*　*　*

The woman next to me on the floatplane
smelled faintly of light.

*　*　*

Kids bootleg some malt liquor from a bum
& one of the boys kisses another
accidentally opening his mouth
on the other boy's cheek. Still there's
no rain, just
telephone poles linked under a blank sky.

*　*　*

Will you tell me about
the staple-sized scars
on your back from an old secret?

*　*　*

Buoy & buoy & bring forth the city's riches,

                                        the
                                        tiniest
                                        locket
                                        or
                                        its
                                        key.

* * *

Parking lots strand you there, just cloudsplit
& properly working engines,
a piece of beer glass, sunlight & pigeons.
Though never birds enough to grind young memories
open on your floor.

* * *

But you'll listen for something.
Shoulders burning. The bicycle torn
in three.

* * *

I check a third time to see if my phone is broken
& the rains set in: weekly downpours,
a fortnight, the twenty-second day, then
a sopping month of monsoons has passed.

* * *

My hands are to me what my voice
must seem to others as I clench my wrist

& watch the neighbor boy finger a sparrow free
from our cat's teeth.

* * *

A moonlight like gauze, no—

* * *

of course it's not, but wouldn't we
want it to be so?
As if that little glow tore open a hole
in your arm & somebody
bandaged you softly up?

Of Bird, String, & Dragging Fables

* * *

In the apple orchard, dragged—
Well . . . somebody did, thick bootsteps
in the bee mud, a dog dead
& carefully scooped away Sunday's
grass heap cuttings & left
the animal to beetles. Carefully
scooped lumps of grass back
over & it was perfect almost. Until
my brother sneaking to meet a girl
heard the raccoons grunting like seals,
pawing the dog's stiff leg out.
My brother with a white Bic lighter.
Raccoon scatter, autumn & count
until forever, then you are done.

* * *

Couldn't you see the ending before it unraveled you?
Would you mind lying down first?
Did you come by foot over the new bridge?

* * *

Here where the poem becomes
                    ladders again,
the little girl returned with candy
& a *nearly* on her lips.

Dirty holdout,
     the bankrobber's melody
   in the evening shower upstairs
           seeps through
               with the hump
     of the ceiling fan
           like the telephone
   into the fury of the vacuum.

Smear
your wet forearm
    over the misted-up mirror.

Bundles of twenties duct-taped
into the busted oven.

Anna steals
out of bed, needs earliness,
    hours of it,
      to reel
 undarkening
landscapes into her old Holga camera: railroad
bridge, garbled depot, plasmabank on South
Fourth Avenue.

This night
someone special
will wander drunk to a crushed payphone
        sink
   the quarter into the gummed slot
   & have
    the conversation anyway.

* * *

Did they last all night in the treehouse?
Exactly what has destroyed your memory?
Did you unscrew this doorknob a little tiny bit like you were asked?

* * *

To pull down: an attic ladder.
Climb it, creakily, up.

* * *

You should really apologize
& bring those dreams into the diner, well . . .
soothed, but with you,
pocketmouse, *ssshhh* . . .

                              exactly so.

* * *

        Sleep it open.

* * *

Exactly so.

* * *

The thieves had lifted
themselves out of the tunnel
with such swiftness—
they rinsed their faces & hands
in the subway washroom,
paused for the clicking turnstile
to click back
& assure a crowded entry just
as the train doors opened, bustling, out.

      * * *

Your soldier hangs his dark uniform
                    neatly in the washroom
            stall & re-enters the city
            in streetclothes.

If it's hung carefully enough somebody will
wear it out & disappear against you,
as you've reappeared yourself
as somebody
somewhere else,
the same . . . but
differently & finished.

* * *

Cities are for
        breaking you into several people
                at once.

    * * *

Swamps however
have white egrets,
noise enough to pull
the eyes out of your head.

    * * *

If drizzle, then
        mosquitoes.

Home almost, at
least where words cut your lip & I spoke
you together & then back apart.

* * *

A fear of all basements & attics,
                    fear of triplets & twins.
                    Fear of trees that lean badly
                    onto powerlines or houses.

* * *

A fear of the sixteenth hour
& flawless numbers.

Of uncles heavy with booze & the hasty games of cousins.
Fear of the telegram & the wires of the doorbell.

* * *

In swimming pool light
the boy who freed the moth
plods back up the stairs, does
a little jig in the mirror
                    & flops
                            into bed.

He has cats & sisters & confuses on purpose
their names.

        * * *

The machines
break down in a street sweeping huff

    & the city has its
                imperial way with us.

The Unofficial Handbook of Librarian Tricks

* * *

Unknowable colors score the railroad crash
& finally the dancer, quick-fingered
with castanets, steps up onto the chair
& flings her red shoes off
each slapping the window onto
the empty courtyard.

* * *

Ghost hole & a wooly rug slung out.

* * *

Anna,
your funny elbows are little crabapples.

You'd better forget the orchard
& the scent of its moist reach.
Forget the *you-know-what* from
                              last night.

* * *

Undressing before a glass of milk.

A telephone requires so much proximity
it almost
defeats the purpose.

* * *

                         Fourteen men
unwind the giant fire hose to begin
    scouring out
        the throat of the train wreck.

* * *

Over the planks.

Unfold it with me, Anna
in the front parlor, but slowly.

* * *

Sleeping on the rug will
                curse us:

(eye sting   bottle of beetles)

Slower, Anna, or we'll reappear.

* * *

Secrets snipped him loose
from his own wrecked robot & hookworm stories.

On the Ferris wheel he counts
all his brothers' missing teeth,
curling his fingers into the mouth of the eldest
& dislodges a penny to
fling it
down to their companions
gazing stupidly up
from below.

* * *

The boy-thieves stretch out the lion's
share on the cardboard box
in the clubhouse.

The most stubborn one they call Hangnail
gets the gumption
   to write it down in his logbook
     & does it patiently
     in the skewered
     light of their forest.

* * *

A white dust of moth-eaten dawn, downy.

* * *

I smack two mosquitoes on you at once,
the side of your neck & thigh, miss both
& fall to the porch slats, laughing.

* * *

The evening call to prayer touched the air open
delicately like a spoiled orange.

* * *

Men who smooth their white slacks,
a thin trace of leather & goat. Gold at the edges
of their lips & strings of tobacco wedged in their teeth.

* * *

I pack a bag absently.

* * *

Nobody's silence but my father's is a comfort to me.

* * *

Toward the coast of
black tea & rain.

* * *

Smog murk, faint shadows, fried tripe on the street
& the color yellow
linger just about everywhere.

*   *   *

Was there too much yeast in the recipe?
Did you find the books of your vilest enemy?
Was the elevator the only part of the building that caught fire?

*   *   *

Then Francis comes home to find
a plain old petty thief
at the fat window, sort of just
casually lurking around & says
you should take off your clothes
& have a drink & a bath & supper
around the corner with me, maybe
a few more drinks (certainly) & fall
in love & have tea, another bath, get
dressed & stop drinking so much, have some
eggs, though, enough with the pills already
& let me kiss your elbows & knuckles
good afternoon & goodbye.

* * *

With turtle shells & cigars
tucked into their jeans pockets,
boys swim on the opposite side
of the lake
from where they found
the missing horse.
Looped a winch hook around its belly,
through the saddle & dragged it ashore,
the rider's boots
still jammed in the stirrups.

* * *

                         Here is
where I sat as it began to snow
& here is a picture of it.

* * *

Then constructed new stories
to pull each other's old ones to pieces.

* * *

Phonebooth & rain spatter & calls
from the dead in the middle of the night.

* * *

Could you re-hide the note I hid inside your steering wheel?
Who fell down the flight of stairs without me?
Did nobody's dog follow you properly home?

* * *

Power-outage librarian tricks & termites
in the book bindery.

* * *

These are all the rooms of the house where I'm not supposed to lie down.

* * *

My clumsy oar work cuts gills into the lake
as I row out beyond morning's bleached pond murk.
A duck perched on the oar, proof of my
absence.

* * *

Really it's proof
of my never having been there at all.

* * *

The late afternoon wind in my eye unspools another song
& the sweat of its music rubs open a blister
on the edge of my palm.

You, anonymous. Me too
until we also become bodies. Un-vanishing &
vanishing back. The trick of _____ like
my mouth   on your mouth.

                    Hello, skeleton.
Hello, lawnmower. Hello, kite-stuck-in-the-tree.
Hello, sunrise. Goodnight.

Boy-Scatter, the Sleepier & the Sleepiest

If each story
　　　depends on the part
　　　　　the teller forgets . . .

Boy-scatter. Sleeping pill sleep.
A twisted out splinter from my neck in the dream.

One woman kicks another in the bus station waiting area,
raccoons return through the cracks in the fence.

Is this what you meant by forgiveness?
Didn't the sockets do their job?
Were you ready & dressed when they clicked open the trunk?

* * *

Bluish wind & a spell turns
somebody's new gazebo to water.

* * *

Forgetting gets
us into our bodies, tipsy
with lack, tipsy with guessing.

* * *

Chatter & then smoke hang together
in the doorways where people huddle
                              in the rain.

* * *

There must be exercises to
                    adjust your eyes
                    to the yellow of darkness.

* * *

Thief of
the museum's mummies, of
the warped projector & film canisters
we found in the meadow behind the taverns.

A girl I knew plowed fields all night
in Bow, slower than sleep-
walking until the sun creamed
the hilled horizon, rousing the elk
to gallop through it & dimmed out
the headlight of her tractor, green
as a lime. Thirsty bugs, coyote shriek,
damp summer things to dread. She was
so quiet in the morning when
we'd wake for work that I feared my
breathing would be the most awful sound
& held it until she began
to search for clothes & dress before me
in the dark.

The man tears out the page in the phone book
at the pancake house. These aren't even movie
sets. This really is Arkansas.

Black-fisted

tire-swing, bird shatter.

A kiss dried on your
forehead.

A squashed cricket-like smell
of the mismatched mountains above.

Crows crumble the shadows on the porch
& I drift numbly
outside for the last trick of dusk
to stop me.

* * *

Our soup cools & the wind
                          dies without our
            permission.

You will lay down tonight with all your clothes
scattered about you on the roof.

            * * *

Did you say *yes* until it stopped happening?
Were there pieces in the street?
Did anybody see your name in the registry?

* * *

Post Office posters of shrugging thieves who know
the bank tellers, not by name, but by the scent
of their golden perfumes.

Umbrella. The boy takes it
from the hook

on the lavender wall.
Tonight, he thinks, *rain will*

fill the basement . . .
Then he'll shimmy up

the tattered treehouse rope,
rat-like onto its little shingles

& let the storm do to me
what a man can do

to another man in the street.

* * *

Grackles of laughter.
A wet ghost sings her
widower's body shakily
out of his shoes.

* * *

Twin sisters filling the restaurant
with their laughter from
the unattended bathroom. A man shorn
off from the din, hiding in a stall.

* * *

Until the boy is forced to eat his father's cigarette, he
& his brothers row into the center of the river to toss over
the oars.

* * *

The boat flung back from their bodies.

* * *

The second hour to fold in from dusk
scolds me, just loosens more boy-scatter on the roof.

* * *

But the light from my memory
bristles in your eyes

                    onto your red
                    cheeks which
gives the soaked road breeze
a field of flowers to stick to.

* * *

A gospel strain that drills little holes
in your kneecaps.

* * *

Thief of all the other thieves'
ladders.

* * *

The three prisoners escaped into the swamplands.
Bickering kept them
together.

* * *

Hatchet heavy as a baby.

* * *

Another question which starts with the word *if*
brings a man down
like ellipses & a paragraph break.

I go walking, watching for foxes, perpendicular
to the canals.

Hoping you get home (& under
                              the covers)
                  before me.

* * *

Here is the gift
of snow: the way it never seems to come or last
but feels inevitable, even effortless when it does.
& finally foxes, raggedy, the color of copper coins
or whatever is made from copper anymore
that they put into your hand
as they bring you to your feet, send you
          on your way.

The Bowling Alley's Most Beautiful Thief

* * *

Photographing destroys one angle of memory
& reveals this to us.

Christmas or Boxing Day.

Trying all afternoon to stay in bed, or at least
until the light sank below the reservoir towers.

* * *

Here where
the afternoon squanders the balconylight
                & North Italy splits into
        ten thousand & twelve
        roads.

* * *

Then the tram slows to a halt
& grimy boys with taller girls in wool skirts
board the cars with buckets
of daffodils, as if on cue from the sun-kicked field.

* * *

Do you still know about all the chalked-in things happening here?
Would you say it again in different words?
But whose hand was it on your leg in the dream?

Magpies fly out from the cartoon cat's
slippery teeth, I feign exasperation

& the little girl on the sofa scoffs,
calling my bluff, & says,

Oh, yeah right—
        The best part with the cliff
          & the birdcage
    & the rubber hose & that grumpy
old bulldog hasn't even happened yet.

* * *

A loose
smell of vodka with mustard in the motel room.

* * *

That old story of the pregnant woman
stuck in the elevator. Technicians speechlessly
rope themselves into the building's guts.

* * *

Until I put your toe, with its little drop of blood,
into my mouth.

Until you work your fingernails into my lower back
like skin mites.

* * *

Until starlings return & nest in the engine.

Until you win the match point
with speed & integrity.

Until the storms break open the leaf-clogged ravine.

Until night flattens you out
like the screen door of a porch in tricky moonlight.

Until you unstick the kite from the oak's branches.

Until your name finds you in another body.

Triangulated position of girl thieves
in the crossbeams, in the horizontal rafters.
Pulleys & ropes across, clicked into their bellies.

Where blankets become a makeshift door.

* * *

A woods of forgetting,
fathom it by story
& by torch.

* * *

The thief of Lucian's portrait of Francis Bacon.
Amsterdam double thieves who laddered up
to the window & snatched three
van Goghs.

* * *

Cornfield & bloodmash.

* * *

Francis stands upright
     in the middle of tying his shoes
          from the bed
          & begins, mid-yawn,
          to paint.

*　*　*

I like perfect examples:
Vieux Carré & the boy-thief of
the black boat's oarlocks,
of the sparrow eggs in the dock nests.

*　*　*

From the basement I could hear him
dragging the bed around unless
it was raining hard.

*　*　*

What did the cops forget to ask you?
Did your little nap do this to you?
Do you remember the story of the lepidopterist stung nearly to death?

* * *

Storehouse, bike chain, wheel-
barrow, flatiron & the special heft of the body
where there is nothing but
your own dumb arms to carry
you on to Anna's clubhouse.

* * *

Roy says, *thief it*, like a verb, got
thieved or
      torn to bits, bitten
                to squares, tipped
to shit, for drunk.

* * *

I switched my shoes
& thought we were really gonna bowl.
All the boy-thieves laugh like drunk dragons,
one kid spits his grape gum-wad out into
the pitcher of root beer
he's howling so hard.

* * *

Ten pins & a nickel-eyed sharper
hides something
at the bowling alley locker
              where nobody
you knew before had anything
to hide.

* * *

Pumpkin dogs
& a bellyful of sour candy like seawater.

* * *

Shame lifts its fingers off the piano keys.

* * *

Here in the ice rink changing rooms
                         somebody pockets
            a photograph of a girl off the thick
            rubber floor
                    & the ice sweeper keeps us
                                        back, then
                        gives a nod as he
slumps in his seat, lipping a menthol above
the shiny ice.

Lug Your Careless Body out of the Careful Dusk

And though we lose eleven eyelashes a day

by blinking alone we cannot enter

the Kingdom

—Christian Hawkey, "Night without Thieves"

* * *

August haunts me with November, a held-
hug longing for leaf weather

& hot black tea steeping
while the clawfoot
drains back into its silly shape.

* * *

Playing poker, my brother & I
are in the neighbor's velvety basement study.
Teaching me good words by telling me never to
repeat them.

* * *

The painting above us begins to mock our gestures:
                                    Ghost hands appear
from the lacquered table
                        almost
connected to clowns
who hustle the table clean
                    with cigar huff & sneers.

* * *

Was there a way to hide the map before he came in?
Did you recognize the key to the hutch?
Couldn't you find your bicycle in the blizzard?

* * *

The first man to fall asleep today
overheard what we said & took it
all the way in with him.

* * *

Found him against the hedge where it smelled
of peeled potatoes, coffee grinds.
Maggots swarming in the crook
of his arm, he lay there as if
hanging upside down on the earth
his own hat crushed under his head.

* * *

I get sleepy
on bridges.

I get wide
awake when the camera tracks back.

I get pulled into the bushes
the way this frozen pond slipped
my neighbor through the ice.

    * * *

The cloud mass bludgeons the waxy light
& stretches dusk out
              like bad carpet.

    * * *

One candle finds
you in an emptying room.

* * *

A color comes in
to me, a return—
looking around from
the same spot
on the porch,
something on
fire & harmless.

* * *

The boy arrived with a book of penguins
under his arm or tucked in his satchel.
But he found the schoolhouse empty.

* * *

There were no voices or visitors & so he
walked inside, met the janitor with a
surprised look, laughter & then one
of them said the word *what*
twice.

* * *

Couldn't you unwind the phone cord in the dream?
Were the crooks thirsty or true?
Did the padlock sink swiftly to the bottom?

* * *

What did the sign remove you from?
Were there reasons to return without gifts?
Have you been to the northern most coast from here?

* * *

Couldn't they fix you a pancake?
How did the mail arrive in the middle of the night?
Where didn't they find butterflies?

* * *

Soft snow under
the black perfect.

* * *

Twinkle. A word
sometimes met
with burning
planets & eyeholes
of people awake
especially at night
outside maybe
in the snow also.

* * *

Love happens this way—
horses turning to sawdust,
the sun unbuckling your
boots for you.

* * *

Memories (a torn open roof,
taste of marmalade or warm beer,
goldfinch smacked a window
or drawn into a book with three
kinds of color & some black)

find us stopped in a doorway kissing
or whistling, pulling that door shut,
or a shirt off, a sliver out, a page
loose, a sky over,
a melon apart.

* * *

Starcrumble
bad bridges & skiffs in chop.

* * *

You still must keep
at a certain distance
for the whole body to
appear
          in the photograph.

THE IOWA POETRY PRIZE AND EDWIN FORD PIPER POETRY AWARD WINNERS

1987

    Elton Glaser, *Tropical Depressions*

    Michael Pettit, *Cardinal Points*

1988

    Bill Knott, *Outremer*

    Mary Ruefle, *The Adamant*

1989

    Conrad Hilberry, *Sorting the Smoke*

    Terese Svoboda, *Laughing Africa*

1990

    Philip Dacey,

        Night Shift at the Crucifix Factory

    Lynda Hull, *Star Ledger*

1991

    Greg Pape, *Sunflower Facing the Sun*

    Walter Pavlich,

        Running near the End of the World

1992

    Lola Haskins, *Hunger*

    Katherine Soniat, *A Shared Life*

1993

    Tom Andrews,

        The Hemophiliac's Motorcycle

    Michael Heffernan, *Love's Answer*

    John Wood, *In Primary Light*

1994

    James McKean, *Tree of Heaven*

    Bin Ramke, *Massacre of the Innocents*

    Ed Roberson,

        Voices Cast Out to Talk Us In

1995

    Ralph Burns, *Swamp Candles*

    Maureen Seaton, *Furious Cooking*

1996

    Pamela Alexander, *Inland*

    Gary Gildner,

        The Bunker in the Parsley Fields

    John Wood,

        The Gates of the Elect Kingdom

1997

    Brendan Galvin, *Hotel Malabar*

    Leslie Ullman,

        Slow Work through Sand

1998

    Kathleen Peirce, *The Oval Hour*

    Bin Ramke, *Wake*

    Cole Swensen, *Try*

1999

    Larissa Szporluk, *Isolato*

    Liz Waldner,

        A Point Is That Which Has No Part

2000

    Mary Leader, *The Penultimate Suitor*

2001

    Joanna Goodman, *Trace of One*

    Karen Volkman, *Spar*

2002

    Lesle Lewis, *Small Boat*

    Peter Jay Shippy, *Thieves' Latin*

2003

    Michele Glazer,
        Aggregate of Disturbances

    Dainis Hazners, *(some of) The*
        Adventures of Carlyle, My Imaginary
        Friend

2004

    Megan Johnson, *The Waiting*

    Susan Wheeler, *Ledger*

2005

    Emily Rosko, *Raw Goods Inventory*

    Joshua Marie Wilkinson,
        Lug Your Careless Body out of the
        Careful Dusk